Cooking with Ess___ Through t__
Winter Holidays

Healthier versions of traditional (and non-traditional)
drinks, appetizers, desserts, candies and edible gifts

Written & Illustrated by Kerrie Hubbard

Print ISBN: 978-1-64945-094-4

Written, illustrated, and designed by Kerrie Hubbard

Visit Kerrie's website at www.kerriehubbard.com

Disclaimer:

PLEASE PLEASE do NOT ingest any essential oil that is not a pure grade oil safe for consumption. Many essential oils on the market can be harmful if swallowed. If you aren't sure of the quality of the oils you're using, find oils you can confidently use, or substitute powdered spices and extracts (see page 4 of this book for help with that). extracts into the recipe

While I've put every effort into the accuracy of the recipes and information contained in this cookbook, I cannot be held responsible for the outcome of the recipes you use. Please note that while I experiment in the kitchen a lot (and encourage you to do it too), using different ingredients may result in varied results. Other variables such as oven temperatures, brands of ingredients, etc. make it impossible to guarantee your results.

Dedication

It took nearly three years of effort to bring this cookbook to life. So many fantastic people in encouraged me to keep going when I wanted to quit, ate endless amounts of various 'winter' recipes without complaint (even in the summer), gave technical advice, and cheered me on.

I couldn't have done it without their help.

Tanya

Kennifer

Erleen

FO

Booster

Ellen & Susan

Kristina

Goatie

Rich & Velma

Mutti

Vonny

Friday Nite Dinner Girls

The Bean Farm Fam

My dT Team

Table of Contents

Winter Drinks

Sweets

Treats

Gift Ideas

Misc.

Tips for Cooking with Essential Oils

Don't be intimidated if you've never used essential oils in your cooking.
If you keep these tips in mind, you'll be fine!

A little Bit Goes a Long Way

Essential oils are up to 70% more potent than herbs. You don't need very much to add nice flavor to your food. In fact, one drop of peppermint oil contains roughly the same amount of peppermint that is in 28 cups of peppermint tea. Needless to say, a little oil goes a very long way.

Be Conservative

When reading the recipes, the amount of oil listed might be too strong for you. Because of that, it's best to start small, taste and adjust. It's a lot easier to add an extra drop of essential oil than it is to take one away.

Master the Toothpick Swirl

Sometimes the recipe will call for a 'toothpick swirl'. This means you need less than one drop of oil. Simply insert a toothpick through the top plastic orifice of the bottle and dip it into the oil. Take that toothpick and swirl it into the food you're preparing.

Add Oil to a Spoon First

Some essential oils take their time dripping out, but some drop out so quickly it's hard to control them. If you add your oils into your food directly you might get more oil than you wanted. Instead, drop the oil onto a spoon and then stir that spoon into your recipe. This way, if too much comes out of the bottle, you can adjust the amount before adding to your food.

1

Wait Until the Last Possible Moment

When heating your food to a higher temperature, it's best if the essential oils are added last (when possible). Heat can damage the therapeutic value of the essential oil. The same amazing flavor will remain, but the health benefits might be diminished. It's not always possible to do this, but keep it in mind for when it is.

Mix with Fat First

If your recipe calls for any kind of oil, butter, or fat, mix the essential oils into this first. It will help disperse them into the recipe more evenly.

Simmer Overpowering Flavors Down

If when adding an herb oil (Oregano, Thyme, Cilantro, etc.) to your food, you add too much, let the food simmer for a while longer. The flavor WILL mellow and you'll end up with an amazing, complex taste.

Be Adventurous!

Don't be afraid to (cautiously) experiment. Again, go slow (on the amount of oils you start with) and have fun. You can usually very easily substitute most spices in your recipes that have an essential oil equivalent.

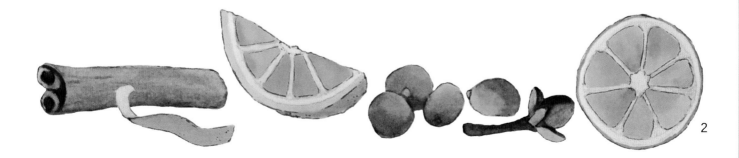

2

Swapping Essential Oils
for Herbs, Fruit & Spices

You might be wondering, 'Why use essential oils when you can just use regular herbs and spices?'

The short answer is: You can. Every recipe in this book is easily adaptable to the common ground (or fresh) spice that is in the kitchen (see the chart on the next page for how to swap spices and essential oils with each other).

However, using essential oils gives you enhanced health benefits. Essential oils, while tasting and smelling similar to the spice alternatives, have a slightly different and much more potent (up to 70% more) chemical makeup than your traditional spices.

Let's take Lemon oil for example.

It takes around 65 lemons to produce a 15mL bottle of Lemon essential oil. Lemon oil is made by a cold-pressed process that extracts the essential oil from the rind of the fruit. While Lemon oil smells like lemon juice, and has a similar taste, its chemical makeup is very different from lemon juice (which is made from squeezing the juice of the fruit from the pulp).

I'll just go a teeny bit science nerd on you for just a second. Don't let your eyes glaze over.

One big difference between Lemon oil and lemon juice is that Lemon oil is very high in a substance called limonene. Limonene is a powerful antioxidant. It supports healthy digestion and respiratory function as well as healthy immune system support. (While there is some limonene in lemon juice, there's a way higher concentration of it in Lemon oil.)

So, if you use Lemon oil in your recipes instead of lemon juice, you'll be benefiting greatly from massively more limonene which helps support a healthy body.

Since essential oils are 50-70% more potent and concentrated than the fresh herb, it also takes a LOT LESS of the oil to create the flavor (and it will give you a lot more health benefits).

Lastly, have you ever been in the middle of making a recipe and realized you don't have an ingredient you need? So frustrating! But by using essential oils in place of fresh herbs, fruits, and spices, you don't have to worry if you're out of lemons or that your rosemary molded in the fridge. You can use your essential oils instead!

(An added bonus: good quality essential oils stored properly will last for many years, even decades.)

As you become more familiar with using essential oils in your kitchen creations, you'll figure out exactly how you like to swap them out.

Below is a general guide to get you started. You can adjust to your own tastes from there. One drop of oil is roughly equal to the following dry/powder ingredients (unless otherwise noted):

Basil, 1 teaspoon	Grapefruit, 1 teaspoon of zest
Black Pepper, 1 teaspoon	Green Mandarin, 1 teaspoon of zest
Cardamom, 1 teaspoon	Lemon, 1 teaspoon of zest
Cassia, 2 tablespoons	Lemongrass, 3 teaspoons
Cinnamon Bark, 2 tablespoons	Lime, 1 teaspoon of zest
Coriander, 1 teaspoon	Marjoram, 2 teaspoons
Cilantro, 1 tablespoon fresh	Oregano, 2 teaspoons
Clove, 2 teaspoons	Peppermint, 1/2 teaspoon extract
Cumin, 1 teaspoon	Rosemary, 2 teaspoons
Dill, 1 tablespoon of fresh	Tangerine, 1 teaspoon of zest
Fennel, 2 tablespoons	Thyme, 2 teaspoons
Ginger, 1 tablespoon	Orange, 1 teaspoon of zest

Peppermint Hot Cocoa

Ingredients:

1 cup coconut milk (or milk of choice)
1/2 cup water
1 tsp coconut oil
1 Tbsp raw cacao powder
1/2-1 tsp real maple syrup (or to taste)
1 drop Peppermint oil
1 drop Turmeric oil
Dash each of salt and cayenne pepper (optional)

Hot Spiced Cider

Ingredients:

1 quart apple cider
5-6 drops Orange oil
3-4 drops Clove oil
3-4 drops Cinnamon oil

Directions (for either):

Add all ingredients to a saucepan and stir to combine. Heat over medium heat, stirring frequently until desired tempertature is reached.

Pour into mug and enjoy.

5

Lavender White Cocoa

1 cup coconut milk (or milk of choice)
1/2 cup water
1 tsp coconut oil
1 Tbsp white cocoa powder or cocoa butter
1/2-1 tsp real maple syrup (or to taste)

1 drop Lavender oil
1 drop Copaiba oil
Dash of salt (optional)
Splash of pure vanilla extract (optional)

Directions:
Add all ingredients to a saucepan and stir to combine. Heat over medium heat, stirring frequently until desired temperature is reached.

Pour into a mug and enjoy.

6

Cardamom London Fog Tea

Ingredients:
Boiling water
1 teabag black tea of choice
1/2 cup oat milk (or milk of choice)*
A toothpick swirl of Cardamom oil (or to taste)
A bit of raw honey to sweeten

Directions:

Add a teabag to a mug and fill your mug half full with boiling water.

While the tea is steeping, add the milk, Cardamom oil, and honey to a small saucepan on medium heat. Stir until ingredients are mixed and the desired temperature has been reached.

Pour the milk mixture into the tea, stir, and enjoy.

*If you'd like your milk frothy, oat milk is best,
7 but if you stir any milk with a wire whisk, that helps too!

Spiced Matcha Latte

Ingredients:

1/2 cup water
1 heaping tsp matcha powder
1 drop Cinnamon oil*
1 drop Turmeric oil*
1 drop Ginger oil*
1 cup milk or milk alternative of choice
Honey to sweeten to taste

Directions:

Add water, matcha powder, and milk to saucepan. Use whisk to combine ingredients. Heat over medium heat to low boil.

Remove from heat, add honey and essential oils. Stir well to incorporate.

Pour into a mug and enjoy.

*If one full drop is too much, start with a toothpick swirl for each oil.

8

Golden Milk

Ingredients:

3 cups coconut milk
  (or milk alternative of choice)
1-2 drops Turmeric oil
1 drop Cinnamon oil
1 drop Ginger oil
1 tsp honey (or to taste)
Pinch freshly ground black pepper
1 tsp coconut oil

Directions:

Combine ingredients in medium saucepan. Heat until warm, stirring often. Let sit for 10 minutes to infuse.

(You'll need to stir this one as you drink it as it has a tendency to want to separate. It's worth the stir!)

Spiced Milk

Ingredients:

1 cup coconut milk
  (or milk alternative of choice)
1 drop Cinnamon oil*
1 drop Ginger oil*
Pinch of cayenne powder
2 Tbsp maple syrup (adjust to your taste)
1 Tbsp almond butter (or other nut butter)

Directions:

Combine in small saucepan until warm and nut butter is melted and mixed together well.

*If a full drop is too spicy for you, start with a toothpick swirl and adjust from there.

Turmeric Latte

Ingredients:

1 drop Turmeric Oil
1 drop Copiaba Oil
1 toothpick swirl Ginger oil
1 toothpick swirl Black Pepper
1 heaping tsp nut butter
1 heaping tsp honey
1 1/2 cups milk of choice

Directions:
Combine together in small saucepan. Heat to desired temperature, stirring regularly.

Cinnamon Latte

Ingredients:
1 tea bag of choice
Boiling water
½ tsp coconut oil
½ cup milk of choice
1-2 drops Cinnamon oil
Honey to taste, optional

Directions:

With teabag in mug, add boiling water, filling up approximately halfway.

Heat milk, honey and essential oils until warm. Add to mug. Stir and enjoy.

Chai Tea

This recipe makes enough to stash it in a jar in the fridge and make your chai tea lattes all week.

Ingredients:
6 cups vanilla oat milk
6 black tea bags
3 drops each Cinnamon and Ginger oils
1 drop each Clove and Cardamom oils
1 drop each Orange and Black Pepper oils
Honey or other sweetener as needed

Directions:
Heat 3 cups of water to boiling. Remove from heat and add tea bags, allowing them to steep, 5-10 minutes.

Add the rest of the ingredients to the saucepan and warm to desired temperature, stirring regularly. Pour into mug and serve warm.

10

Make yourself a warm cup of tea using your favorite herbal tea blend then add a drop or two of a relaxing essential oil (see next page).

Good teas for relaxation are: chamomile, passion flower, or any number of teas on the market blended specifically for relaxation.

(Just remember to drink decaffeinated if you're really trying to relax!)

Put a bit of honey on a spoon (sweeten to taste) and drop the oils into the honey.
Stir into tea and enjoy.

Try some of these oils/combinations:

1 drop Roman Chamomile

1 drop each Peppermint, Lemon and Lavender

1 drop each Orange and Lemon

2 drops Lemon

1 drop Ginger

1 drop Bergamot

12

Healthy Russian Tea

Ingredients:
1 gallon + 2 cups water
4 black tea bags
6 cups orange juice
6 cups pineapple juice
   (buy fresh or use 46 oz can)
4 cups apple juice
½ cup lemon juice
2 drops Clove oil
5 drops Cinnamon oil
½-1 cup coconut sugar
   or honey (optional, to taste)

Directions:
In large stock pot, bring 1 gallon of water to boil. While you wait, add 2 cups of water to a small saucepan and bring to boil. Reduce to low heat and add 4 tea bags. Let tea steep.

Once the gallon of water is boiling, add the fruit juices, and sugar (if you're using it). Stir together, until sugar is disolved. Remove from heat. Pour the tea into this mixture (removing the teabags) and stir in the essential oils.

Taste to see what you need to adjust. You might want to add more sweetener or essential oils.

Keep on low heat and let simmer for a few minutes. Serve hot or cold.

(makes 2 gallons)

Hanukkah Punch

Ingredients:
3 cups water
¾ cup coconut sugar or honey
3 drops Cinnamon oil
1 cup orange juice

Directions:
Make cinnamon syrup by adding 3 cups of water and honey to a saucepan and bringing to a boil over medium heat. Stir regularly.

Reduce to simmer, add Cinnamon oil and allow to simmer for 10 minutes.

Serve warm or cold.

(serves 30)

Homemade Ginger Ale

Make Simple Syrup:
6 drops Ginger oil
6 drops Lemon oil
4 cups water
1 cup coconut sugar or honey

Directions:
Bring water to boil, dissolve honey into water. Remove from heat. Add essential oils. Cool completely.

Store in sealed glass container in fridge for up to 1 week.

Make Ginger Ale:
1/4 cup ginger simple syrup
2 cups sparkling water, seltzer, or club soda.

Add ice, if desired.
Stir and enjoy.

14

How to Make a Holiday Smoothie

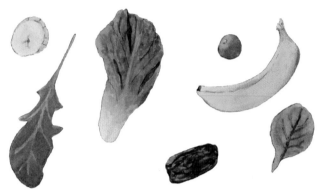

Base Ingredients:

Add these base ingredients to a blender then pick a smoothie flavor to finish.

1-1 1/2 cups coconut, almond or other milk
1 scoop protein powder
1/2 - 1 frozen banana
1-2 cups greens (kale, swiss chard, romaine, spinach, etc.)

Gingerbread Cookie Smoothie

To the base ingredients, add:
1 Tbsp molasses
3 pitted dates
1 Tbsp Cinnamon oil
1 drop Ginger oil
Toothpick swirl to 1 drop Clove oil

Chocolate Peppermint Smoothie

To the base ingredients, add:
1 Tbsp cocoa powder
1 drop Peppermint oil

Apple Pie Smoothie

To the base ingredients, add:
1 apple
6 almonds
1 -2 drops Cinnamon oil
1 drop Lemon oil

15

Carrot Cake Smoothie

To the base ingredients, add:
1 carrot
1-2 drops Cinnamon oil
6 walnut halves
1/4 cup pineapple

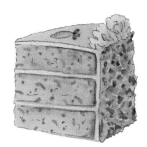

Pumpkin Pie Smoothie

To the base ingredients, add:
1/2 cup pumpkin puree
1-2 drops Cinnamon oil
Toothpick swirl to 1 drop Clove oil
1 drop Ginger oil
5 pecan halves

Cranberry Orange Smoothie

To the base ingredients, add:
1/2 cup pomegranate juice
1 orange (peeled)
2 Tbsp fresh cranberries
6 walnut halves
3 drops Orange oil

16

Mocktails for Everyone

Most of these simple recipes just require shaking or stirring the ingredients together for a quick special drink.

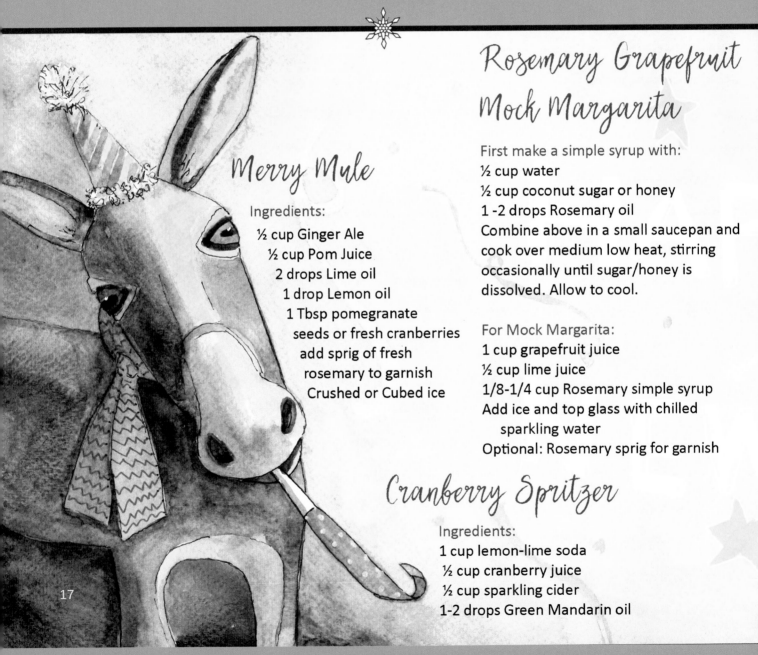

Rosemary Grapefruit Mock Margarita

First make a simple syrup with:
½ cup water
½ cup coconut sugar or honey
1 -2 drops Rosemary oil
Combine above in a small saucepan and cook over medium low heat, stirring occasionally until sugar/honey is dissolved. Allow to cool.

For Mock Margarita:
1 cup grapefruit juice
½ cup lime juice
1/8-1/4 cup Rosemary simple syrup
Add ice and top glass with chilled sparkling water
Optional: Rosemary sprig for garnish

Merry Mule

Ingredients:
½ cup Ginger Ale
½ cup Pom Juice
2 drops Lime oil
1 drop Lemon oil
1 Tbsp pomegranate seeds or fresh cranberries
add sprig of fresh rosemary to garnish
Crushed or Cubed ice

Cranberry Spritzer

Ingredients:
1 cup lemon-lime soda
½ cup cranberry juice
½ cup sparkling cider
1-2 drops Green Mandarin oil

17

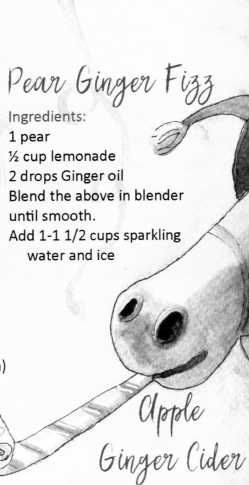

Pear Ginger Fizz

Ingredients:
1 pear
½ cup lemonade
2 drops Ginger oil
Blend the above in blender
until smooth.
Add 1-1 1/2 cups sparkling
    water and ice

Plum Thyme Prosecco

First make a simple syrup:
½ cup coconut sugar or honey
½ cup water
2 drops Thyme oil
Bring to a boil, remove from heat, let
cool. Chill until ready to use.

Then assemble:
2 plums, peeled and chopped
3 cups lemon-lime soda (or use
    sparkling water for a less sweet option)
Juice from one lemon

Muddle the plums, simple syrup
and lemon juice until juicy. Divide
this between two glasses and pour
over crushed ice. Top off with
soda/sparkling water. Stir.

Garnish with plum slices and/or fresh
sprigs of thyme (optional).

Apple Ginger Cider

Ingredients:
½ cup spiced apple cider
½ cup Ginger ale
2 drops Lemon oil
Ice

18

Grandma's Fruit & Brandy Cookies

Every year without fail, Grandma baked these cookies, put them in a Christmas tin, and shipped them off to me. These cookies embody the taste and smell of nostalgic childhood Christmas to me. The secret is adding a bit of brandy and letting the flavors mingle together overnight. While Grandma's original recipe called for candied fruit, I've swapped dried fruit instead and cleaned up the recipe a little, making it just a bit more healthy while maintaining the flavor that reminds me of the holidays more than any other.

Ingredients:

1 cup coconut oil (or butter)
1 cup brown coconut sugar
1/2 cup honey
2 eggs
1 tsp baking soda
1 tsp salt
1 tsp vanilla
2-3 drops Cinnamon oil
2 1/2 cups flour blend of choice
1 cup EACH pecans and walnuts
  (coursely chopped)

1 cup EACH of raisins, dried pineapple and
  dried cherries (coursely chopped)
    (or substitute 3 cups dried fruit of choice)
1 cup brandy*

*If you'd rather not use alcohol in your recipe, add 3 tsp brandy extract to a 1 cup measurer, add half a cup of apple juice. Top with water to make full cup.

Directions:

Cream softened coconut oil with mixer then add sugar, honey, and eggs. Mix well.
Add other ingredients in order given.
Add brandy a little at a time.
Cover and refrigerate overnight.

Preheat oven at 325°F
Scoop dough into rounded spoonful and place on baking sheet. Bake about 18 minutes.
Store in airtight container.

Shortbread Cookies

Ingredients:
1 cup almond flour
1/2 cup arrowroot powder
1 tsp vanilla
1/3 cup maple syrup
1/3 cup coconut oil
5-7 drops Lemon oil
1 toothpick swirl Ginger oil

Directions:
Sift dry ingredients together. Mix wet ingredients together. Add the wet ingredients to the dry. Form into a ball, cover and stick in fridge for 30 minutes.

Roll dough out between two pieces of parchment paper. Cut out using small cookie cutters, or cut into squares and poke holes in dough with fork.

Bake at 325°F for 15 minutes (don't overcook). Let cool before removing from cookie sheet.

Gingerbread Shortbread Cookies

It's easy to turn the above recipe into a gingerbread rendition. Here's all you need to do:

Follow above recipe EXCEPT:

Instead of 1/3 cup maple syrup, use 1/3 cup molasses

Instead of 5-7 drops of Lemon oil, use 5-7 drops Orange Oil

Instead of toothpick swirl of Ginger oil, use 2 drops Cinnamon oil and 1 drop Ginger Oil

Pecan Pie Thumbprint Cookies

Filling:
1/3 cup dates, chopped
5 Tbsp maple syrup
1/4 cup coconut oil
1 Tbsp coconut milk (or milk of choice)
1/2 tsp vanilla extract
1/8 tsp salt
1 1/2 cups pecans, chopped

Cookie:
2 1/4 cups almond flour
1/4 tsp salt
1/4 tsp baking soda
5 Tbsp coconut oil at room temperature
3 Tbsp maple syrup
1-2 Tbsp coconut milk
1 tsp vanilla extract
4-6 drops Lemon oil

Directions:

Pour 1 cup of hot water over dates and let sit for at least 10 minutes. Drain and place in blender.

In saucepan, heat maple syrup, coconut oil, coconut milk and vanilla over low heat. Add warmed ingredients, plus Lemon oil to dates in blender. Blend until smooth. Pour into bowl, add chopped pecans and stir to mix. Set aside.

Preheat oven to 350°F. Line cookie sheet with parchment paper.

In mixing bowl, combine almond flour, salt, and soda. Whisk in coconut oil until mixture is crumbly. Stir in maple syrup and vanilla. Add coconut milk a little at a time. (Add just enough to keep the dough from crumbling.)

Roll dough into balls (about 1 1/2 tablespoons in size). Place balls on cookie sheet and flatten slightly. Create an indention in middle with thumb (to hold filling).

Add mound of filling to center of each cookie and bake for 12-14 minutes. Allow to cool on cookie sheet before removing to keep them from falling apart.

Thumbprint Variations

Instead of pecan pie filling, add a mound of raspberry (or other flavored) fruit jam in center of cookie.

For a chocolate variation, add 1 Tbsp raw cacao to the cookie mix (adjust the moisture with the coconut milk to make the dough the right consistency).

22

Pumpkin Pie Thumbprint Cookies

Ingredients:

1 cup almond flour (or flour of choice)
1 tsp cornstarch
3/4 tsp baking powder
1/4 tsp salt
1 1/2 Tbsp coconut oil
    or butter, slightly melted
1 egg at room temperature
1 1/2 tsp vanilla extract
1/2 cup coconut sugar

Filling:

1/4 cup pumpkin puree
2 drops Cinnamon oil
1 drop Ginger oil
1 toothpick swirl Clove oil
    (OR substitute all essential oils for
        3 drops Protective oil blend*)
1 Tbsp maple syrup or agave

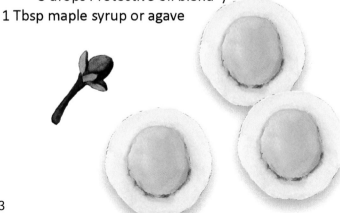

Directions:

For cookies, whisk all dry ingredients together in small bowl. In larger mixing bowl, beat together butter, egg, and vanilla. Stir in sugar. Add flour mixture. Stir until blended.

Place in fridge for 20 minutes.

While cookie dough chills, prepare the pumpkin filling. Stir together all ingredients and place in plastic baggie and set aside.

Preheat oven to 350°F and line cookie sheet with parchment paper.

Roll cookie dough into 24 balls. Using thumb, make indent in center of each cookie.

Take baggie of filling and snip off one corner of bag (to make a piping bag) and fill each center with filling.

Bake for 8-10 minutes. Allow to cool for 10 minutes before removing them from cookie sheet.

23

If you don't have Protective blend, see page 55 for recipe to make your own.

Molasses Cookies

Ingredients:
2 cups almond flour
1/4 cup arrowroot powder
8 Tbsp cassava flour
   (or you can sub out for more almond
   flour)
1 large egg, beaten
8 Tbsp butter or coconut oil, melted
1/3 cup honey
1/3 cup molasses
3 drops Cinnamon oil
3 drops Ginger oil
1/2 tsp salt
coconut sugar for rolling

Directions:
Preheat oven to 375°F
Mix all dry ingredients together.
Mix all wet ingredients together.
Combine the two and let dough sit for
5 minutes.

Roll dough into balls. Roll balls in sugar.
Place on parchment lined cookie sheet
and bake for 12 minutes. Cool 10 minutes
before removing.

Tip: if cookies flatten out too much when
baking, add a bit more almond flour to your
mix before baking next batch.

Apple Pie Cookies

Ingredients:
1/3 cup grated or finely minced
   apple (peeled)
4 Tbsp coconut oil
4 Tbsp honey or maple syrup
1 tsp vanilla extract
1 1/2 cups almond flour
1 Tbsp arrowroot powder
1 Tbsp flax seed meal
1/2 tsp baking soda
1/4 tsp salt
2 drops Cinnamon oil
1 drop Lemon oil
Dash of powdered nutmeg
   (optional)

Directions:
Preheat oven to 350°F
Combine all ingredients together,
being careful not to over-mix dough.
Cover and refrigerate 30 minutes.

On a parchment lined cookie sheet,
place mounds of cookie dough,
flattening slightly.

Bake for 15 minutes. Let cool before
removing from cookie sheet.

24

Holiday Mug Cakes & Pies

Sometimes a cake or pie for one is exactly what's called for...warm, comforting, and just for you alone. Mug cakes (and pies) give you just enough of the taste of the holidays without the fear of overindulgence. These cakes pretty forgiving and therefore are easily adjustable to most food sensitivities so don't be afraid to experiment with different flours, oils, and other additions.

Mug cakes are traditionally cooked in the microwave (fast and easy) but I prefer the oven. (Make sure you're using an oven safe mug, bowl or ramekin.)

Mix all recipe ingredients together and if using microwave, cook for 1 1/2 to 3 minutes (depending on wattage of oven) or cook at 350°F in regular or toaster oven for 12-18 minutes or until done.

Pear Ginger Cake

Ingredients:
1/2 a ripe pear, peeled and diced
2 Tbsp water
Mix the two together and
    cook until pear is soft.
Drain water.

1 Tbsp molasses
3 Tbsp almond flour
1 1/2 Tbsp coconut flour,
    arrowroot, or cassava flour
    (or flour of choice)

Add:
1/2 to 1 egg
1 tsp butter or coconut oil

1 drop Cinnamon oil
1-2 drops Ginger oil

Chocolate Candy Cane Cake

Ingredients:
3 Tbsp almond meal   1 egg
3 Tbsp raw cacao or   dash of salt
    cocoa powder   1 drop Peppermint oil*
2 Tbsp honey   a sprinkle of crushed candy
1 tsp vanilla   canes on top (optional)

*use a drop or two of
Cinnamon oil instead of
Peppermint oil and make a
Mexican hot cocoa cake!

25

Pecan Pie Cake

Crust:
1 tsp butter or coconut oil
2 Tbsp almond flour
dash of baking powder and salt
Mix ingredients together and press
into bottom of mug.

Filling:
1 Tbsp melted coconut oil
1 tsp date or coconut sugar
1 Tbsp agave
1 egg, beaten
1/2 teaspoon vanilla
3 Tbsp chopped pecans
1 Tbsp raw cacao

2 drops Cinnamon oil
1 toothpick swirl Cardamom oil
 dash of salt

Not Yo' Grandma's Fruit Cake

Ingredients:
1/4 tsp butter or coconut oil, melted
1 egg
1 Tbsp honey
1 Tbsp molasses
1/4 tsp vanilla
1/4 tsp brandy (or brandy flavoring)
3 Tbsp almond flour

1 1/2 Tbsp coconut flour, arrowroot
   or cassava flour (or flour of choice)
3 Tbsp dried fruit (cherries, pineapple,
   raisins, cranberries, figs, dates, etc), chopped
1 Tbsp chopped pecans
2 drops Cinnamon oil
1 drop Ginger oil
2 drops Orange oil

26

Snowman Cake Pops

Traditionally, cake pops are made by baking a sheet cake that you cool and crumble up before mixing frosting into the crumbles to create a new 'dough'. This is then rolled into balls, frozen for a bit (to make them more stable), then dipped into a candy coating. Using this common method would definitely work to create snowmen cake pops (just use your favorite cake and frosting recipe and follow the steps below to add 'snowman decorations', etc.).

However, below is a mostly raw, healthier alternative to the traditional cake pop (but still super tasty!).

For cake:
1 cup raw cashews, soaked overnight
Up to 1 cup of water
   (to use as needed for proper consistency)
8 dates, soaked for 15 minutes in hot water
      1 1/2 tsp vanilla extract
      2 tsp chai seeds
      8 drops Lemon oil

For decorating and 'frosting':
1/2 cup cacoa butter
1/2 cup raw cashews, soaked overnight
1 drop Turmeric oil
4 drops Lemon oil
2 tsp honey

Small candies, fruit leather, black frosting gel, etc. for decorating lollipop sticks

Stick pretzels for arms (if you add these, they need to be eaten soon because the pretzel gets soft if you store them too long)

To make cake:
Drain off water from both cashews and dates. Add all ingredients (reserving some of the water back) to a food processor or good blender and blend until it resembles course crumbs. Add water as necessary to get consistency. (It should be crumbly, but able to hold together when you roll it into a ball.)

27

Lemon Brownies

These 'brownies' get their name from their moist, dense, brownie-like texture.

Ingredients:

3/4 cups butter or coconut oil, softened
1 1/8 cups almond flour (or flour of choice)
3 eggs
3 Tbsp lemon juice
6-8 drops Lemon oil
1 1/8 cups coconut sugar (or sugar of choice)
1/2 tsp salt

Frosting:

2 cups coconut cream, room temperature
1/2 cup tapioca starch
1 Tbsp honey, slighly warm (pourable)
1/2 tsp vanilla

Directions:

Preheat oven to 350°F
Grease 8x8 pan and set aside.

With an electric mixer, blend flour, sugar, salt, and butter until combined. In separate bowl, mix together eggs, lemon juice, essential oil and butter/coconut oil until combined. Pour the wet mixture into the dry mixture and beat at medium speed for 2 minutes, until smooth and creamy.

Pour into 8x8 pan and bake for 23-25 minutes (the edges should be golden brown).

Allow to cool and then frost.

For Frosting:

Scoop out the thick coconut cream and reserve the liquid (if desired) for another purpose.

In a mixing bowl, combine all ingredients except for the tapioca starch. Beat on medium speed until combined.

Gradually add tapioca starch until frosting reaches desired consistency. Mix until smooth. Store in refrigerator until ready to use.

32

Chili Lime Nuts

Ingredients:

¼ tsp garlic powder
2 drops Lime oil
½ tsp onion powder
2 Tbsp lime juice
1 tsp chili powder
½ tsp paprika

1 tsp sea salt
2 Tbsp olive oil
2 cups almonds

Directions:

Preheat oven to 350°F. Mix ingredients together with almonds and let them soak in bowl for 15 min. Spread on cookie sheet. Bake 25 minutes, stirring every 5 minutes.

Spicy Skillet Nuts

Ingredients:

2 cups mixed nuts
1 tsp chili powder
1 drop Cumin oil
1 drop Black Pepper oil
½ tsp sea salt
1 Tbsp olive oil

Directions:

Heat up cast iron pan over medium heat. Add nuts, stirring regularly until lightly browned. Coat nuts with olive oil, then coat with spice mixture.

Stir an additional 2 or 3 minutes before removing from heat. Let cool.

Rosemary Thyme Nuts

Ingredients:

3 cups roasted, lightly salted nuts
2 Tbsp olive oil
2 Tbsp coarsely chopped fresh rosemary leaves
1/4 tsp cayenne pepper
1 Tbsp coconut sugar
1 tsp kosher salt

1 drop Thyme oil
1 drop Cumin oil
1 drop Black Pepper oil

Directions:

Preheat overn to 300°F. Mix oils and seasonings together in medium bowl.

Add nuts and stir until well coated. Sprinkle with sugar and salt and stir again. Transfer to baking pan with sides. Bake 15 minutes, stirring after 10.

Let cool. Store in airtight container.

34

Gingerbread Spiced Nuts

Ingredients:
1 egg white
1/2 cup coconut sugar
1 Tbsp kosher salt
1 pound raw mixed nuts pecans,
    walnuts, cashews, almonds, etc.
1 1/2 tsp ground allspice
3/4 tsp ground nutmeg
1 drop Clove oil
2 drops Cinnamon oil
2 drops Ginger oil

Directions:
Preheat the oven to 325°F. Line two baking sheets with parchment paper.

In a large bowl, whisk the egg white until it foams into small, evenly sized bubbles, about 3 minutes. Add the coconut sugar, essential oils, spices, and salt to the egg white and whisk until incorporated. Add the nuts and mix until completely coated.

Spread the nuts between the two parchment lined baking sheets in an even layer. Transfer to the oven and roast until dry and golden brown, 40 minutes.

Halfway through, remove the pans from the oven, stir the nuts with a rubber spatula, then return to the oven to finish roasting.

Remove the nuts from the oven allow them to rest on the baking sheets for 10-15 minutes. Transfer to a sealed container, and keep for up to 5 days.

Cinnamon Roasted Almonds

Ingredients:
1 16 oz package raw almonds
    (or nuts of your choice)
3 Tbsp water
3/4 cup coconut sugar
2 tsp vanilla
1 1/2-2 tsp powdered cinnamon
5-10 drops Protective oil blend*
    (add slowly and taste to make sure you
    get the right amount for your own tastes)

Directions:
Preheat oven to 250°F. Line a baking sheet
with parchment paper

In medium bowl, add all ingredients
(except nuts) and stir. Stir in the nuts,
making sure to coat them well. Let sit a few
minutes until some of the moisture has
absorbed and the sugar has dissolved.

Spread onto the baking sheet and bake for
60-70 minutes (until the nuts are crunchy)

*If you don't have Protective blend,
see page 55 for recipe to make your own.

Dark Chocolate & Sea Salt

Ingredients:
2 cups raw, unsalted almonds
3 1/2 oz dark chocolate chips
1/2 cup raw cocao or cocoa or carob
powder
1/2 cup coconut sugar
1 Tbsp himalayan sea salt
4 drops Orange oil

Directions:
Melt dark chocolate in microwave or using a
double-boiler on stovetop. Stir in Orange oil.
Add almonds to mixture and coat well.

In a separate bowl, add cocoa powder, coconut
sugar and sea salt. Stir to combine.

Add a few chocolate covered almonds at a time
to the cocoa mixture and coat with the
powdered mixture (don't add all almonds at
same time or you'll get a mess).

Place on a baking sheet lined with parchment
paper to let them 'dry' out.

Store in fridge in covered container.

36

Quinoa & Cashew Bark

Ingredients:
1/4 cup quinoa, rinsed
1 Tbsp coconut oil
1/2 cup chopped cashews
    (or nuts of choice)
1 tsp sea salt
Dash of cayenne pepper (optional)
3-5 drops Copaiba oil
3 1/2 oz dark chocolate bar

Directions:
Heat pan to medium heat and add coconut oil and quinoa. Cook, stirring often, until quinoa is golden brown (5-8 minutes). Remove to medium bowl and add all other ingredients (except for chocolate).

Melt chocolate in double boiler. Pour melted chocolate over other ingredients and stir together. Spread onto parchment to cool. Break into pieces to serve.

Dark Chocolate Bark

Ingredients:
8 oz dark chocolate bars
Nuts, seeds, dried fruit of choice
6-8 drops Orange oil
    (OR 2-4 drops Cinnamon oil)

Directions:
Chop chocolate bars into small pieces. Place in a double boiler and melt chocolate over medium-high heat, stirring frequently.

While chocolate melts, chop assorted nuts, seeds and berries coursely.

Once chocolate is melted, spread onto parchment paper. Sprinkle with assorted toppings while chocolate is still warm.

Let set on counter until cool, or pop in fridge to speed up the process.

Peppermint Bark

Ingredients:
4 oz unsweetened baking chocolate
1/4 cup coconut oil
1/4 cup honey
6-8 drops Peppermint oil

Directions:
Melt chocolate and coconut oil together in a double boiler, on medium-high heat. Once melted, remove from heat, add honey and essential oils, and mix together.

Line 8x8 baking dish with parchment paper.

Pour the chocolate mixture into the baking dish and freeze for 1-2 hours.

Once totally hard, break into pieces to serve. Store in fridge.

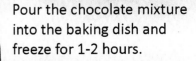

Pumpkin Spiced Buckeyes

Ingredients:

3/4 cup creamy nut butter
1/4 cup pumpkin puree
2 cups powdered sugar
dash of salt

4 Tbsp butter or coconut oil, softened
1 cup semi-sweet chocolate chips
1 drop Protective oil blend*
1 drop Cinnamon oil
1 toothpick swirl Ginger oil

*If you don't have Protective blend, see page 55 for recipe to make your own.

39

Directions:

In mixer, mix together peanut butter, pumpkin puree, and butter/oil until creamy. Add all other ingredients (except chocolate chips) and combine well.

Cover bowl and refrigerate for 30-60 minutes. Scoop cooled dough by tablespoon and roll into balls. Place on parchment and refrigerate 20 minutes.

In double boiler, melt chocolate chips. With toothpick, dip balls into chocolate, leaving the top exposed. Store in refrigerator in sealed container. Makes 20-25 balls.

Chocolate Mousse

Ingredients:
Two 13 1/2 oz cans coconut milk (not light)
1/2 cup honey
2 tsp vanilla extract
4 tsp kosher bovine gelatin
6 Tbsp cacoa powder (or cocoa powder or carob powder)
1-2 drops Cinnamon oil (or essential oil of choice)
pinch of salt

Directions:
Heat milk and honey until warm. Remove 1/4 cup of mixture and pour into a small bowl. Add the gelatin to the bowl and stir well. Allow to sit for 3 minutes, then pour all ingredients together and stir until smooth.

Pour into small cups or ramekins and place in the refrigerator for 1-2 hours before eating.

Peanut Butter Cups

Ingredients:
1/2 cup coconut oil, slightly melted
1/2 cup cacao powder (or cocoa or carob powder)
1/2 cup peanut butter (or nut butter of choice)
1/4 cup honey
1/2 tsp vanilla extract
2 drops Copiaba oil or oil of choice

Directions:
You can make these by using candy molds or mini muffin tins (lined with papers).

Blend together all ingredients but don't overmix. (It will be runny, but don't worry, it won't stay that way!)

Pour into candy molds or mini muffin tins lined with papers. Place in fridge/freezer to set.

These store best in covered container in fridge or freezer.

Chocolate Truffles

For truffle inside:

3/4 cup chocolate chips or chopped dark chocolate

3/4 cup cacao powder (or cocoa or carob powder)

1/2 cup coconut cream

2 Tbsp coconut oil

1/2 cup smooth nut butter of choice

1 tsp vanilla extract

1/3 cup pure maple sugar (or coconut sugar, although it will be a bit more grainy)

1/4 tsp salt

1-2 drops Cardamom or Ginger or Cinnamon oil or combination (or use 4-6 drops of either Pepper mint, Lemon, Orange oil, etc.)

For outside shell:

3/4 cup chocolate chips or chopped dark chocolate

3/4 cup cacao powder (or cocoa or carob powder)

1 1/2 tsp coconut oil

For toppings (optional):

Finely chopped nuts of choice

Shredded coconut

Directions:

Starting with the truffle insides, melt the chocolate and cacoa powder together with coconut cream over low heat, stirring constantly until melted together. Remove from heat and stir in nut butter, sugar, vanilla, essential oil, and salt. Once very smooth, refrigerate for about 15 minutes (until you can easily roll into balls).

Line cookie sheet with parchment paper. Roll mixture into balls (work quickly while it's cool). Chill balls for an additional 15 minutes.

While balls chill, prepare outside shell by heating ingredients together over low heat, stirring constantly until melted and smooth. Let cool slightly before dipping balls into chocolate mixture.

After dipping, sprinkle with toppings, if desired. Store in air-tight container in refrigerator.

Easy No-Cook Fudge

Make chocolate or peanut butter fudge (or both!)

Ingredients:

1/2 cup coconut oil, melted

3/4 cup cacao powder (or use powdered peanut butter instead for peanut butter fudge)

3/4 cup protein powder

1 cup chopped nuts (or 1 cup chocolate chips for peanut butter fudge)

6 drops Peppermint or Orange oil for chocolate fudge (or 2 drops Cinnamon oil for peanut butter fudge)

Directions:

Mix all ingredients together and press into an 8x8 pan. Chill for 1 hour before cutting into squares.

Spicy Chai Caramel Corn with Honey

This caramel corn is out of this world! There are just enough spices to make it extra delicious without putting it over the top. Plus, it's sweetened with honey instead of corn syrup. Everyone I've given this to loves it. Because of that, it makes a great, unique gift...if you can bear to part with it!

(And bonus points: You don't even need a candy thermometer to make it!)

Ingredients:

1/2 cup unpopped popcorn
(you want to end up
with around 15 cups of popped corn)
1/2 cup coconut oil or butter
1/2 cup honey
pinch of salt
1/4 tsp baking soda

1/2 tsp vanilla extract
4 drops Cinnamon oil
2 drops Cardamom oil
2 drops Ginger oil
1 drop Black Pepper oil

Directions:

Pop the popcorn and set it aside.

Melt coconut oil/butter with the honey, sugar and salt in small saucepan. Bring this *almost* to a boil, stirring constantly. Turn down heat and let gently simmer, stirring, for about 5-ish minutes.

Remove from heat. Stir in the vanilla, soda, and essential oils. They'll foam up when you add them, but just stir it down (use a wooden spoon).

HELPFUL TIPS:

Add the 1/2 teaspoon vanilla to a 1 teaspoon measurer and add the essential oils in with it so it's all ready to dump at once.

This stuff gets hard fast, so work quickly...also, it will seem like not enough gooey stuff for the amount of popcorn you have, but you'll be pleasantly surprised to see it's the perfect amount once you're done!

I throw it all into my turkey roasting pan and place it into the oven for 30 minutes at 250, stirring every 5-10 minutes. Watch it so it doesn't burn. The baking time is just to make it less sticky. (You can also use cookie sheets, if you don't have a roasting pan.)

As soon as it's cool enough to handle, break up the larger chunks, if you want. Enjoy warm or cold. Store in airtight container.

44

Essential Oil Infused Honey

Local honey paired with essential oils is a perfect blend of flavor and sweetness with a double boost of health.
A small jar of infused honey makes a perfect gift.
For best flavor, add the essential oils several days before using or gifting.

The quantity of oil suggested below is for 1 cup of honey. Adjust to your personal tastes.
(Store in a glass container with tight fitting lid.)

Pumpkin Spice Honey

10 drops Cinnamon oil
4 drops Ginger oil
2 drops Cardamom oil
1 drop Clove oil

Spicy Chai Honey

6 drops Cinnamon oil
6 drops Ginger oil
2 drops Cardamom oil
1 drop Black Pepper oil

Lemon Honey

12 drops Lemon oil
4 drops Lime oil

Cinnamon Honey

12 drops Cinnamon oil
4 drops Orange oil

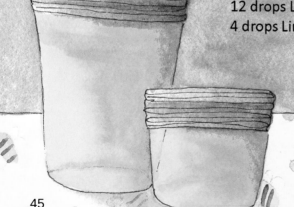

Gingerbread Honey

6 drops Ginger oil
4 drops Orange oil
4 drops Cinnamon oil
1 drop Clove oil

Turmeric Ginger

6 drops Turmeric oil
6 drops Ginger oil
4 drops Wild Orange oil

Candy Cane Honey

10 drops Peppermint oil
4 drops Orange oil
dash of vanilla extract

46

Homemade Marshmallows

If you've never had homemade marshmallows, you're in for a treat! The store-bought variety doesn't even come close to these. Plus, they're made with honey and maple syrup without any refined sugar at all!

Ingredients:

arrowroot (or powdered sugar)
1 cup cold water, divided
2 1/2 Tbsp powdered kosher bovine gelatin
1 cup real maple syrup (dark is better)

1/4 cup honey
pinch of salt
1 tsp vanilla extract
2-4 drops essential oil of choice
      (Protective Blend*, Cinnamon, Orange, etc.)

*If you don't have Protective blend,
see page 55 for recipe to make your own.*

Directions:

Line an 8x8 pan with parchment paper. Cover bottom and sides of pan and leave a little sticking out on top (for easier grabbing out later).

Sprinkle the parchment lightly with either arrowroot powder or powdered sugar (this will keep it from sticking).

Add 1/2 cup of cold water to a mixing bowl (a stand mixer works really great for this recipe, but you can use a handmixer as well) and sprinkle the gelatin over the top.

Place 1/2 cup water in a saucepan with the maple syrup, honey and salt. Cook over medium heat and bring to a boil. Once it comes to a boil STOP STIRRING IT (no matter how much you're tempted to do it)! Watch it carefully at this point because it can easily boil over (if it starts, turn down the heat a bit).

When sugar is boiling, use a candy thermometer to take the temperature. You'll need to get this mixture to 'soft ball stage' which is between 240-243F. This should take 10-15 minutes. Once you reach the right temperature, turn off the heat.

Turn mixer on low (with the whisk attachment in place if you've got a stand mixer) and slowly pour the hot sugar syrup into the water and gelatin mixture.

47

Once all the syrup is in the mixing bowl, turn speed up to medium and mix for about a minute, until the mixture starts to turn a bit lighter. At this point, add vanilla extract and essential oils. Turn speed up to medium-high and whisk for another 5-10 minutes, until the mixture turns into marshmallows.

(You'll be able to tell they are ready when the mixture has about tripled in size, is no longer warm to the touch, and holds a bit of its shape.)

If you haven't mixed it enough, the marshmallows won't set up, too much, and they will harden so fast you won't be able to get them out of the bowl fast enough.

Once they're ready, act fast! They will want to start setting up immediately and you've only got about 30 seconds to transfer them to your prepared 8x8 pan.

Smooth out the top with a spatula and let set on counter for 4 hours before cutting them.

Remove the block of marshmallow from the pan (by pulling on the parchment) and setting on top of a cutting board.

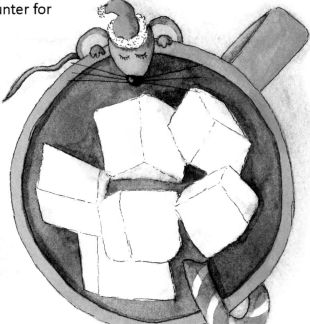

Sprinkle more arrowroot on top of the marshmallows (to help with cutting) and use either a really sharp knife or a pair of scissors to cut into small squares.

After they're cut, roll them around in more arrowroot or powdered sugar (so they don't stick to each other). Once they're all coated, dump them into a colander and shake off excess powder. They keep for about a week (store in freezer for longer).

Drink Mixes

Who doesn't like a warm, comforting drink in the winter? That's why drink mixes are the perfect gift.

Mix up a batch or two of one (or all) of the mixes here, pour them into a mason jar, add a tag and a bottle of Peppermint or Cinnamon oil (for the hot cocoa mixes), and you've got a great gift!

49

Hot Cocoa #2

If you'd rather give a cocoa mix that already contains milk (or a milk alternative), add 1 cup of powdered milk or powdered coconut milk to the traditional cocoa mix recipe.

Add these directions:

Add 2-3 tablespoons of cocoa mix to 1 cup hot water. Add one drop of essential oil. Stir and enjoy.

Traditional
Hot Cocoa Mix

Ingredients:
1/2 cup raw cacao powder
(or carob powder or cocoa powder)
1/2 cup semi-sweet chocolate chips
1 cup coconut sugar
1 tsp vanilla powder
1/2 tsp salt

Directions:
Blend the chocolate chips and sugar in a blender until they are a fine powder. Add all other ingredients and stir well.

Store in air-tight jar and add the following directions:

Warm up 1 cup of milk of choice, add 2-3 Tbsp of mix and 1 drop of essential oil. Stir & enjoy!

Chai Concentrate

Ingredients:
10 black tea bags
4 cups water
2 teaspoon vanilla extract
4 drops Cardamom oil
4 drops Cinnamon oil
2 drop Clove oil
2 drop Black Pepper oil

Directions:
Bring 4 cups of water to a boil and remove from heat. Add the tea bags and let steep for 15 minutes.

Remove tea bags, add essential oils and vanilla. Stir and pour into glass jars with tight lid.

Attach these instructions:

Mix chai concentrate 50/50 with milk of choice. Heat and enjoy.

Snowman in a Jar

While this isn't technically a 'food' item, it's a fun and inexpensive gift idea (and you CAN eat it, if you want!) I've included both my long-time tried and true original recipe for playdough, as well as a gluten free alternative for those that are super sensitive to gluten.

Part of the fun with this project is to collect bits and pieces that will become part of the snowman kit--little twigs and pebbles, buttons and little strips of fabric, etc. Anyone I've given a snowman in a jar kit to has used it for hours (and sometimes YEARS) of old-fashioned creative entertainment! Who wouldn't want an indoor snowman party?

What You Will Need (makes 2 kits):

2 recipes of homemade playdough of choice

2 empty jars with lids (Mason jar, recycled nut butter jars, etc.--you'll want them about 2 cup size)

Essential oils (I like Peppermint for snow and Orange for noses, but pick your favorites!)

Twigs, buttons, tiny rocks, scrap material (for scarves), etc.

Black acrylic paint (optional) to paint tiny rocks for 'coal' eyes

Snack-sized plastic bags or small pieces of plastic wrap

Glue stick or string (to add label, if desired)

Paper to make or print label

Assemble:

Stick one batch of playdough 'snow' in bottom of jar, wrap 'nose' playdough in plastic wrap and stick on top, add rest of snowman parts to top of jar, screw on lid and glue or tie on label.

Traditional Playdough

Ingredients:

1 cup white flour
1/2 cup salt
1 Tbsp cream of tartar
1 Tbsp cooking oil of choice
1 cup water
1-3 drops essential oil
orange food coloring
clear or white glitter (optional)
(to add the sparkle in the 'snow'.*)

Directions:

Heat up oil in saucepan. Add flour, salt, cream of tartar, and water. Stir until mixture forms soft ball (3-5 minutes). Remove from heat and knead dough several minutes.

If you're adding essential oils and/or glitter, do it at this point.

Remove a small piece of dough for nose and add a drop or two of orange food coloring and essential oil.

Place in snowman jar per instructions.

Gluten Free Playdough

Ingredients:

2 cups plain, instant
    mashed potato flakes
1 cup cornstarch
1/2 cup salt
1 cup hot water
1/2 cup white vinegar
2 1/2 Tbsp oil
orange food coloring
1-3 drops essential oil

Directions:

Combine potato flakes and corn starch in large bowl. Add water, vinegar and oil. Mix well for several minutes. (The longer you mix it, the stretchier it becomes.)

Follow same instructions as regular playdough for the nose, glitter, and essential oils.

Holiday Diffuser Blends

If you love your home filled with the scents of the holiday season (even when you're not cooking anything delicious), diffuser blends are the perfect solution. Not only will they fill the air with nostalgia, they're healthy for you too (unlike most commercially scented products on the market). Simply fill your diffuser with the oils suggested and enjoy the aromas of fresh baked pies, gingerbread cookies and more. Mmmm- It might make you hungry!

Warm Apple Pie

2 drops Cinnamon oil
2 drops Ginger oil
1 drop Clove oil

Spiced Chai Latte

3 drops Cardamom oil
1 drops Cinnamon oil
1 drop Clove oil
1 drop Ginger oil
1 drop Black Pepper oil

Orange Pomander

4 drops Orange oil
1 drop Cardamom oil
1 drop Clove oil
1 drop Rosemary oil

Candy Cane

3 drops Peppermint oil
2 drops Invigorating oil blend*
1 drop Siberian Fir oil

Hot Spiced Cider

4 drops Gathering oil blend*
2 drops Orange oil

Christmas Cookies

3 drops Protective oil blend*
2 drops Invigorating oil blend*
1 drop Peppermint oil
1 drop Lime oil

Spicy Orange Vanilla Cupcakes

6 drops Metabolic oil blend*
4 drops Invigorating oil blend*

Aside from putting them in your diffuser, here are some gift ideas: Add one of the recipes below to a 2 oz spray bottle, fill with water and a splash of witch hazel for a holiday room spray. Use to scent gift bags, cloth ornaments, and homemade sachets.

Make hanging car air fresheners out of felt or cardboard and gift with a mini bottle of one of the blends.... the ideas are endless!

Flannel Blanket

3 drops Grounding oil blend*
2 drops Orange oil
2 drops Bergamot oil

Evergreen Wreath

3 drops Siberian Fir oil
1 drop Cedarwood oil
1 drop Peppermint oil
1 drop Rosemary oil

Winter Wonderland

3 drops Siberian Fir Oil
3 drops Cypress Oil
1 drop Sandalwood Oil
1 drop Eucalyptus Oil

Putting up the Tree

4 drops Peaceful Holiday oil blend*
1 drop Peppermint oll
1 drop Orange oil
1 drop Arborvitae oil

Hygge Home

3 drops Restful oil blend*
2 drops Peppermint oil
1 drop Invigorating oil blend*

Peace and Joy

2 drops Joyful Holiday oil blend*
2 drops Grounding oil blend*
1 drop Frankincense oil

54

DIY Oil Blend Substitutions

Don't have the oil blend listed in the recipe? Here's some approximate substitutions for the oil blends in this book:

Protective Blend

The Protective blend is found in many of the recipes in this book because it's made up of all the good smells and tastes of the holiday season. This recipe is an approximation of the Protective Blend and makes enough to fill a 5mL glass bottle so you'll have plenty to make and use for any recipes in this book.

Protective Blend Recipe:
20 drops Clove oil
20 drops Lemon oil
15 drops Cinnamon oil
8 drops Eucalyptus oil
5 drops Rosemary oil

The following oils blends are found in some of the diffuser recipes. Use a drop or two of each oil or as needed.

Gathering Blend

Cassia oil
Clove oil
Eucalypus oil
Cedarwood oil
Cinnamon oil

Restful Blend

Lavender oil
Cedarwood oil
Ylang Ylang oil
Marjoram oil
Roman Chamomile oil
Vetiver oil
Sandalwood oil
Splash of pure vanilla extract

Invigorating Blend

Grapefruit oil
Lime oil
Lemon oil
Tangerine oil
Bergamont oil
Clementine oil
Mandarin oil
Orange oil
Splash of pure vanilla extract

Grounding Blend

Spruce oil
Franincense oil
Blue Tansy oil
Blue Chamomile oil
Osmanthus oil

Joyful Holiday Blend

Siberian Fir oil
Orange oil
Clove oil
Cinnamon oil
Cassia oil
Douglas Fir oil
Splash of pure vanilla extract

Peaceful Holiday Blend

Siberian Fir oil
Grapefruit oil
Douglas Fir oil
Himalayan Fir oil
Frankincense oil
Vetiver oil

I hope this cookbook inspires you to get in the kitchen with your essential oils and start experimenting. Why not add healthy oils to your food that will enhance the taste while giving your body a big boost of a lot of good-for-it stuff.

Need Coordinating Gift Tags?

Are you going to give any of these holiday recipes as gifts? I've got you covered! Hop on over to my website and download my free labels and gift tags that go with the recipes in this book. They're formatted for you to easily print from your home printer.

Get yours here: www.kerriehubbard.com/winter-cookbook-labels

Get the Highest Quality Essential Oils

If you want to experience increased health from using essential oils in your food, it's imperitive that you use a pure grade, food safe oil. Most of the essential oils on the market these days are NOT safe to ingest.

Use the URL below to get a wholesale discount on the best oils on the market. Don't take a chance, if you don't know for sure the quality of the oils you're using.

www.eo4you.com

Have questions? Shoot me an email here: Kerrie@kerriehubbard.com

There are no minimum orders or requirements at all.
Zero. Zip. No Risk!

Love this Book?

Contact me here for bulk discounts:
kerrie@kerriehubbard.com

If you bought this book on Amazon, I'd love for you to leave a review.
Thank you!

Kerrie

www.kerriehubbard.com